The First Book of The Antarctic

Personnel of Operation Deep Freeze admire the frigid beauty of the Antarctic from the top of Observation Hill. The men stand in silhouette against the white slopes of Mt. Erebus, some 40 miles distant. Cross has been erected to the memory of polar explorer Captain Robert F. Scott and his party who died in 1912 on their return trek from the geographic south pole. (US Navy)

The First Book of the

ANTARCTIC

Revised Edition

by Rear Admiral
JOSEPH B. ICENHOWER
USN (Ret.)

illustrated with photographs

Franklin Watts, Inc.
845 Third Avenue
New York, New York 10022

SBN 531-00468-6

Library of Congress Catalog Card No.: 56-7431
Printed in the United States of America
4 5 6

Contents

The First Book of The Antarctic

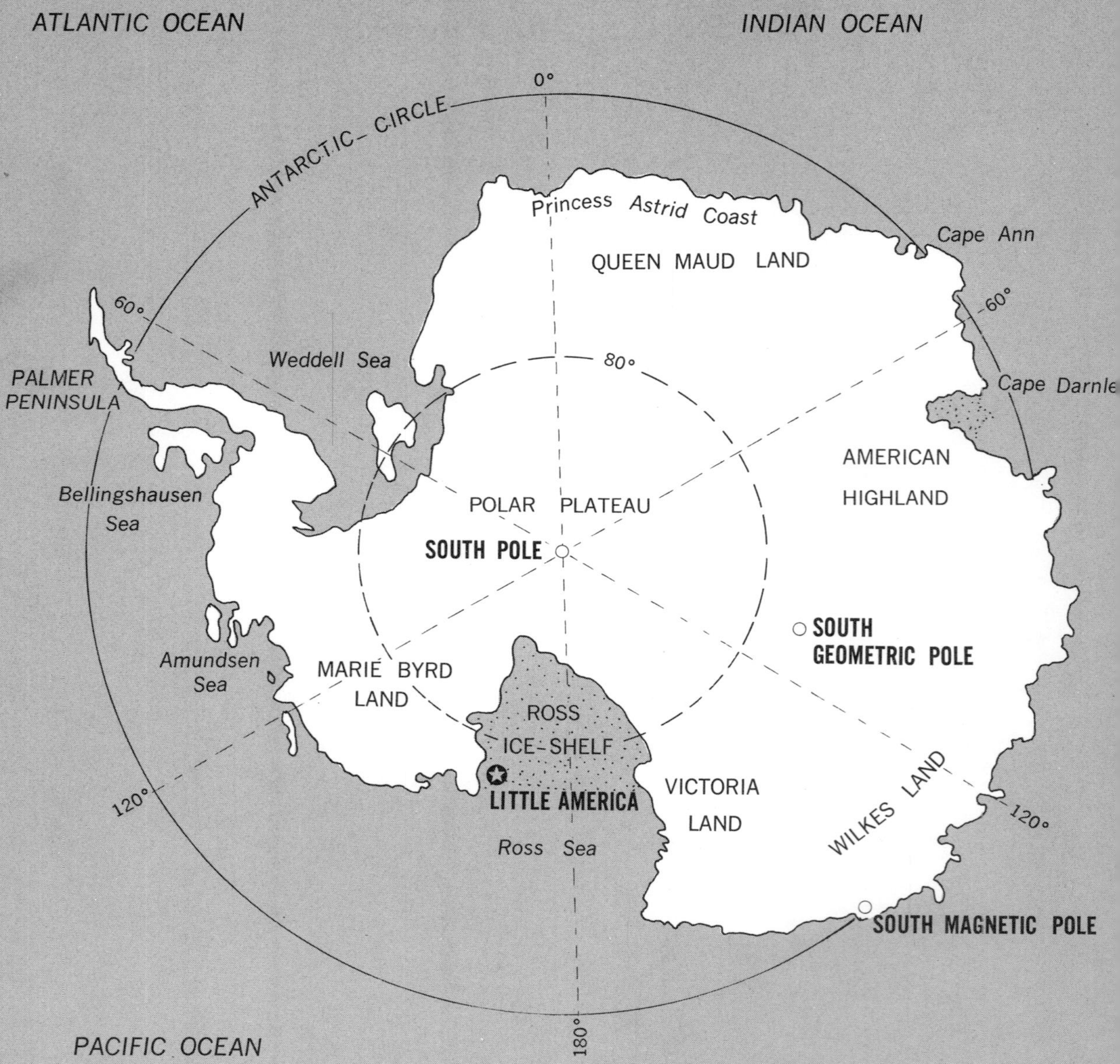
ATLANTIC OCEAN
INDIAN OCEAN
0°
ANTARCTIC CIRCLE
Princess Astrid Coast
Cape Ann
QUEEN MAUD LAND
60°
60°
Weddell Sea
80°
PALMER PENINSULA
Cape Darnle
AMERICAN HIGHLAND
Bellingshausen Sea
POLAR PLATEAU
SOUTH POLE
SOUTH GEOMETRIC POLE
Amundsen Sea
MARIE BYRD LAND
ROSS ICE-SHELF
LITTLE AMERICA
VICTORIA LAND
WILKES LAND
120°
120°
Ross Sea
SOUTH MAGNETIC POLE
PACIFIC OCEAN
180°

The Secret Land

Down at the bottom of the world is the last unexplored continent on this planet — Antarctica. It is covered with ice and snow, and in only a few places does it extend above the Antarctic Circle, an imaginary line extending around the earth at latitude 66°30′S. No one knows exactly what the continent would look like if all the ice and snow were removed from it, although it is certain that there would be a vast landmass of some 5½ million square miles — an area about the size of the United States and Mexico combined — plus many small islands. The Antarctic Ocean which surrounds the continent is actually created by the flowing together of the southernmost parts of three great oceans — the Atlantic, the Pacific, and the Indian.

Millions of years ago Antarctica was green with forests. Its climate was somewhat like that of northern California today. Great animals walked and swam in its swamps. Today there are almost no plants in Antarctica, for the continent is in the middle of an ice age. Except for a few mountain peaks and exposed rocks, it is completely covered by a cap of ice and snow that in some places has been measured at 14,000 feet — or over 2 miles thick. This ice cap represents 95 percent of the world's permanent ice.

No continent in the world is so cold. Only on the icy shore does the temperature ever rise to the freezing point of 32 degrees Fahrenheit. At the Soviet Union's Vostok Station a low temperature of *minus* 126.9°F. was measured. This is the lowest temperature ever recorded anywhere in the world.

These lofty Antarctic mountains, an extension of the Shackleton Range, were discovered as late as 1964 in uncharted areas of Queen Maud Land. (US Navy)

The seasons are reversed in Antarctica. When it is summer in the Northern Hemisphere, it is winter in the South Polar regions. August and September are the coldest months, and during these months the sun never shines. There is continual night.

No land is so windy. Winds up to 200 miles an hour have been registered on anemometers — instruments for measuring wind speed. Winds of 100 miles an hour are common on the Antarctic coast south of Australia.

No continent is so high. Antarctica's central plain rises to nearly 10,000 feet above sea level.

Great mountain ranges hold back the ice cap that covers the interior of the continent, keeping the central portion a frozen wasteland. From the passes between the mountain ranges, great rivers of ice up to 20 miles long spill out into the sea, forced to such movement by the weight of the ice cap on the central plateau. These rivers of ice are called glaciers when they are in the mountain valleys, and when they spread out over the sea they are called ice shelves. The Ross Ice Shelf is the largest in the world and covers an area about the size of California.

The air over Antarctica is the purest in the world. It has a greater proportion of oxygen and nitrogen than other planetary air. But the weather in Antarctica is almost always bad. True, there are a few good days with bright sunshine, but these are rare. Hurricane winds drive the blinding snow across the high plateau until the snow spills out over the ice-clogged sea. When the wind dies down briefly between blizzards, much of the land and the surrounding sea is fogbound. At such times, travel by either land or sea is extremely dangerous. It is dangerous by land because the

An H-34 Seahorse helicopter flies along the Meserve Glacier in Antarctica. (US Navy)

A huge tabular iceberg in the Weddell Sea. Berg was photographed during Operation Deep Freeze in 1956. (US Navy)

traveler may fall into a deep, hidden crack, or crevasse; by sea, because the huge icebergs blend with the fog and are almost invisible to approaching ships.

Mountainous seas and hundreds of miles of thick sea ice guard the secrets of Antarctica. Icebergs several miles long break off the great cliff of ice known as the Ross Ice Shelf to drift northward into the Pacific Ocean. These tabular bergs are so called because they are as flat as tables. They are a mixture of snow and ice called *névé* that has been packed down by the pressure of its own weight into a solid mass of ice. In 1927 a ship sighted a tabular berg 100 miles long and 130 feet high. Because there is roughly six times as much of an iceberg below water as there is showing above the water, this berg must have extended about 1,000 feet below the surface of the sea.

Other icebergs look like great white hills standing up above the sea. They are called ice-island bergs because many Antarctic explorers first thought that they were snow-covered mountains.

Here and there around the continent are smaller icebergs of a blue-green color. These are "glacier" icebergs that have broken off the glaciers or rivers of ice that spill into the sea.

All around the big icebergs are smaller pieces of ice about the

Three Navy icebreakers push together to move a huge berg from the channel of broken ice leading to McMurdo Station, Antarctica. Bits of broken ice called brash *surround the berg. (US Navy)*

Icebreakers clearing the way through the ice pack to McMurdo Station. (US Navy)

size of a medium-sized house. These "bergy bits" have either broken off the glaciers or are made by a large berg's "calving" — the sailors' word for the breaking up of an iceberg. The even smaller pieces of ice, about the size of an automobile, are called brash.

The ice "pack" which surrounds the continent is made of large, flat pieces of ice of various thicknesses known as pans. When the pans have great quantities of water between them they are known as a loose pack. When they are crowded so closely together that they are forced to ride up on top of each other, they are said to be consolidated. Then the sea is ragged with ridges and blocks of upended ice. On a cloudy day the reflection of the great ice pack makes a yellowish white glare in the sky that can be seen for miles. Sailors call it an ice blink.

So dangerous are the waters around Antarctica that Admiral Byrd named them the Devil's Graveyard.

Why Go to Antarctica?

Fridtjof Nansen, the great Norwegian Arctic explorer, once explained why he and others kept risking their lives to explore the

Operation Deep Freeze men look over last year's ice breakup at Scott Base, Antarctica, in the vicinity of Ross Ice Shelf. (US Navy)

forbidding Arctic regions. He said: "Man wants to know, and when he ceases to do so he is no longer man."

Many of the earlier explorers journeyed to the Antarctic for that very reason. Not only did they want to see it for themselves, they were haunted by the idea of a vast southern continent that appeared in the legends of the ancient Polynesians.

Today men go to Antarctica to study the earth, the space around it, the life existing in that part of the world, and to find answers to the earth's historio-geologic past.

Those persons primarily interested in the Antarctic continent are the geophysicists, sometimes called earth scientists because they study the earth and the forces that affect it. The range of these studies include oceanography, meteorology, geology, upper atmosphere physics, and glaciology. Other scientists interested in this polar region are biologists and cartographers (map makers).

In recent years, as a result of their research in Antarctica, meteorologists have collected much valuable information concerning the earth's weather. For example, the cold mass of air over the Antarctic ice cap decides most of the weather for the great areas south of the equator, including South America, Africa, Australia, and the oceans between them. The weather in these parts of the world, in turn, affects weather all over the earth.

Cold air weighs more than hot air, and around the South Pole in the center of Antarctica the greatest mass of cold, heavy air in the world builds up on the polar plateau. When this frigid air roars northward off the continent toward the warmer air over the ocean, the resulting storms can be the worst in the world. Sometimes, when these high continental winds are funneled through

Marine biologists at work in a new biology laboratory at Little America. (US Navy)

the mountain passes, the winds become even stronger. Such high-energy storms cause weather changes that are felt over much of the world south of the equator.

When an earthquake occurs in Antarctica, the great ice pack shifts its tremendous bulk. This affects the level of the seas that wash the warmer world and causes weather changes all over the earth. The United States has built permanent weather stations where meteorologists study and interpret weather information gathered in the Antarctic. There are many semipermanent weather stations, and the scientists have made wide use of weather satel-

A meteorologist checks a multiple anemometer system at Little America. (US Navy)

lites and automatic weather stations powered by atomic power. These weather stations can operate for ten years, often being placed in remote areas. Thanks to the weathermen in Antarctica, their fellow weathermen all over the world will someday be able to make much more accurate predictions.

In Antarctica, meteorologists also hope to learn more about the circulation of air around the earth, how heat processes operate in the air, and what happens to water vapor in the atmosphere. In addition, they hope to gain more knowledge about those puzzling high velocity winds called jet streams that circle the earth high in the upper air; about storms in the upper air that affect worldwide radio communications; and about cosmic rays that bombard the earth from space. They also hope to learn more about the earth's magnetic field.

A variety of minerals and a few semiprecious stones have been found in the very little open ground that exists in Antarctica. Coal, copper, iron, and titanium have been located, and black and red garnets. Scientists believe that there are great treasures of oil and other natural resources yet to be found. They base their belief on the theory that the mountain ranges of Antarctica are an extension of the mountain ranges of North and South America. In both the Rocky Mountains of North America and the Andes of South America valuable minerals have been mined for years. It is reasonable to suppose that buried under the millions of tons of ice and snow these same minerals may exist in Antarctica. If they do, and if a way can be found to get them out, they will help to enrich the world.

Geologists are presently studying one of the most fascinating theories of continent formation yet to be undertaken by man. Many scientists believe that millions of years ago, Africa, South America, Australia, India, and Antarctica were all joined together in one huge landmass. This great landmass was called Gondwanaland, and over the years it broke apart to form the continents as we now know them.

Glaciologists are studying the ice formations in Antarctica which will give them a clue to the great Pleistocene Ice Age in our own hemisphere some 10,000 years ago. By drilling sample cores out of the great ice sheet they can determine what the weather conditions probably were several thousands of years ago. More important, however, they seek to determine whether the ice sheet is melting or building up, because should the ice sheet begin to melt it will change the weather of the whole world and affect the levels of oceans.

Physicists studying the earth's atmosphere are constantly trying to determine what effect sunspots and other space disturbances have on radio communications here on earth. As changes take place in the earth's magnetic field, one can see them in the northern and southern lights of the polar regions. These *auroras* are caused by the *solar wind* — radiation particles emanating from the sun that penetrate our upper atmosphere and come into contact with the earth's magnetic field.

Biologists have been able to identify the various species of the comparatively few plants in the Antarctic, and have been kept busy studying all life ashore and afloat, from bacteria to whales.

Breaking the Trail to Antarctica

Two hundred years ago much of the world believed that beyond the Antarctic ice pack lay a warm, green land inhabited by strange tribes of peoples.

In 1830, a man named Jeremiah Reynolds made a trip in a whaling ship to the waters of Antarctica. He believed that at the South Pole there would be an entrance to the inside of the earth.

He convinced so many people of this that some twenty bills were introduced in Congress proposing to send a naval expedition to the South Pole for the purpose of entering the earth and making friends with the inhabitants who supposedly lived there.

For years stories like Reynolds' had been told by seamen throughout the world. It was not until the middle of the eighteenth century, when the British sea captain James Cook sailed completely around Antarctica, that scientists could even guess at the size of the continent.

Land itself was not discovered until an American whaling captain, Nathaniel Palmer, sighted it in 1820. Palmer Peninsula, due south of South America, is now named in his honor.

As soon as Palmer's discovery was known, many expeditions were fitted out to explore the Antarctic. Russian, American, British, Norwegian, and French sailors and whalers caught sight of the coast and nearby islands.

Just a few months after Captain Palmer sighted Antarctica, Captain John Davis of New Haven, Connecticut, sent a boatload of men ashore to look for seals. This was not known until a few years ago when the captain's logbook was found. Thus, Americans were the first men ashore on the great white continent.

After 1895 there began the great period of Antarctic exploration that gave the world some of its most courageous explorers. It was the time of Sir Ernest Shackleton and Captain Robert Scott from England, of Roald Amundsen from Norway, and Admiral Richard E. Byrd from the United States.

Amundsen and Captain Scott staged one of the most famous races in history. In 1911 both explorers started for the South Pole.

The famous British Antarctic explorer Sir Ernest H. Shackleton commanded an expedition in 1907–9 that located the South Magnetic Pole and penetrated to within 97 miles of the geographic pole. On a later expedition, when his ship Endurance *was crushed by ice (below), Shackleton led his men to safety on Elephant Island. From there he and five companions sailed an open boat nearly 800 miles to South Georgia Island in 1916. After a fatal illness on his last voyage to Antarctica six years later, Shackleton was buried on South Georgia Island. (Charles Phelps Cushing)*

These two men were experienced polar explorers. It was Captain Scott's second journey to the Antarctic, and Amundsen was experienced in Arctic explorations.

Scott was a captain in the British navy. His courage had made him the idol of many schoolchildren in the British Empire. These same schoolchildren raised money to enable him to buy sturdy little Manchurian ponies to draw the sleds he used in his explorations of the South Pole. In addition to these ponies, Scott took some motor tractors with him.

Amundsen's expedition was much smaller and simpler than Scott's. He took dogs to pull his sleds. He had used them in the Arctic and found them excellent. Amundsen and his men dressed like Eskimos, in parkas — outer garments made of fur. They planned to eat pemmican, the trail food of the Eskimos. Pemmican is meat that has been dried and pressed hard, and to which melted fat, raisins, and sugar have been added. As the trip progressed, Amundsen planned to kill the weaker dogs for food. He laid out every detail of his trip beforehand, with advance depots and cairns — high piles of snow — so that he would not get lost on the way back. He planned to strike south from Shackleton's old camp on the Ross Ice Shelf and head straight into the unknown expanse of snow and ice.

Scott, too, worked out every detail of his trip in advance. He planned to travel over the same route Sir Ernest Shackleton had used years before when he had tried to reach the South Pole.

Scott had a terrible trip. His ponies, one hitched to each sled, proved hard to handle. In deep snow they sank to their bellies and could not move. The little animals suffered badly from the cold.

A portrait of the ill-fated Antarctic explorer Captain Robert F. Scott, who with four comrades perished in January, 1912. Before his final dash to the Pole, Scott had made his main camp at Cape Evans on McMurdo Sound. Below, the interior of Scott's hut at Cape Evans has been partially restored. (Charles Phelps Cushing; US Navy)

Weeks before Scott reached his destination they had all either died or had to be killed.

When Scott's little party reached the South Pole they found the Norwegian flag flying there and a small tent left behind by Amundsen's men. It was a terrible blow. Scott and his four companions hitched themselves to their one remaining sled and started back.

Amundsen returned to his base in good health, but Scott's party fought blizzards and terrible surface conditions all the way back. One man died, then a second. Finally Scott and his two remaining companions were pinned down in their tent by a blizzard. There they died.

The early Antarctic explorers were brave men drawn to the frozen continent by love of adventure and the fascination of unknown places. Their story is one of ships being crushed in the ice pack, of terrible blizzards, of suffering and starvation in the icy wastelands. But they broke the trail for the great naval expeditions of later years and for the men at work in Antarctica today.

In 1928, 1933, 1939, and 1946, Admiral Richard E. Byrd led four great expeditions to the Antarctic. He established his camp, Little America, on the Ross Ice Shelf near Amundsen's deserted camp. From there he flew an airplane over the South Pole to drop the American flag. With a brave man's regard for courage, he also dropped the British and Norwegian flags in tribute to Scott and Amundsen.

Admiral Byrd is largely responsible for the world's scientific interest in Antarctica today. In 1934 he spent five months all alone, deep in the Antarctic wastelands, making weather obser-

Admiral Richard E. Byrd is shown here before the takeoff from Little America in 1929 for the South Pole flight. He holds a U.S. flag weighted with a stone from the grave of Floyd Bennett, his pilot on the North Pole flight. Byrd dropped the flag at the South Pole, together with British and Norwegian flags, in tribute to the explorers Scott and Amundsen. (National Archives)

vations. Although he was not the first man to take an airplane into the Antarctic, he proved its effectiveness there. In recent years all Antarctic expeditions have taken planes with them. Admiral Byrd was the first to establish radio communications with the outside world from a base in the polar regions, and the first to make use of the scientific equipment available to explorers today. Indeed, he set the pattern for today's great scientific exploration of Antarctica.

In 1939, Congress authorized the establishment of the U.S. Antarctic Service expeditions under the command of Admiral Byrd. This marked the beginning of large-scale government support for research, and the plan was to man permanent stations year round on the continent. Unfortunately, World War II broke out just after the stations were established, and the government withdrew all the men for the duration.

But activity resumed in 1946–47, when a U.S. Navy Task Force of thirteen ships — including a submarine — literally attacked the

The monument erected to Rear Admiral Richard E. Byrd in Antarctica. (US Navy)

The main camp area of Williams Air Facility, McMurdo Sound, Antarctica. (US Navy)

continent with four thousand men, under the code name of Operation Highjump. Since that time, the United States has maintained permanently manned stations every year in Antarctica.

Naming the Geographic Features of Antarctica

Conflicting claims to various segments of Antarctica have led to a number of geographic features having two or more names. Generally speaking, geographers and historians have been content to adapt the names of prominent physical characteristics as bestowed by explorers. In parts of the white continent, however, national pride has asserted itself. A prime example is the Antarctic Peninsula south of Cape Horn.

Nathaniel Palmer, although the first to sight Antarctica, and specifically this peninsula, did not put his name to the land. Admiral Bellingshausen, leading a Russian expedition, named it Palmer Land after a chance meeting with Palmer in the ice floes north of the area. The British declare that ten months before Palmer's discovery, Captain Edward Bransfield of the Royal Navy discovered the land, and eleven years later John Biscoe named the land Graham Land, after the then-first-lord of the admiralty.

In 1948 the Chileans began to press their claim to the Palmer Peninsula and they named it O'Higgin's Land, after one of their greatest military leaders.

While there are other examples of ambiguity, for the most part the original names of first-order geographic features have stuck. Explorers generally give names to these features to honor their sovereigns, such as Queen Maud Range, Victoria Land, George V Coast, and so forth. It was quite natural for early explorers to

NATIONAL CLAIMS: *Several countries claim portions of Antarctica, but none of these are recognized by the United States. The Antarctic Treaty of 1959 allows men of all countries to travel freely in Antarctica.*

MAJOR EXPLORATIONS: *In 1772, Captain James Cook, a British explorer, began his search for a southern continent. Though Cook sailed around Antarctica and was the first to cross the Antarctic circle, he never sighted the continent. In 1840, an American naval officer, Lieutenant Charles Wilkes, sailed 1,500 miles along the Antarctic coast; Wilkes Land is named after him. Amundsen (1911) and Scott (1912) were the first two men to reach the South Pole. In 1957-58, the Commonwealth Trans-Antarctic Expedition, led by Sir Vivian Fuchs and Sir Edmund Hillary, traveled 2,158 miles across Antarctica, by way of the South Pole.*

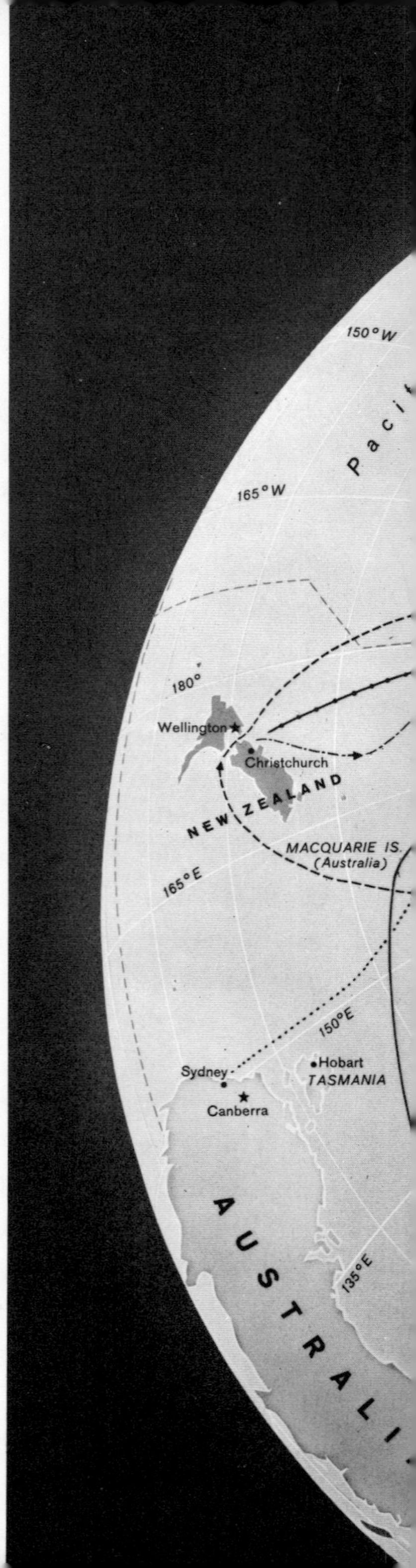

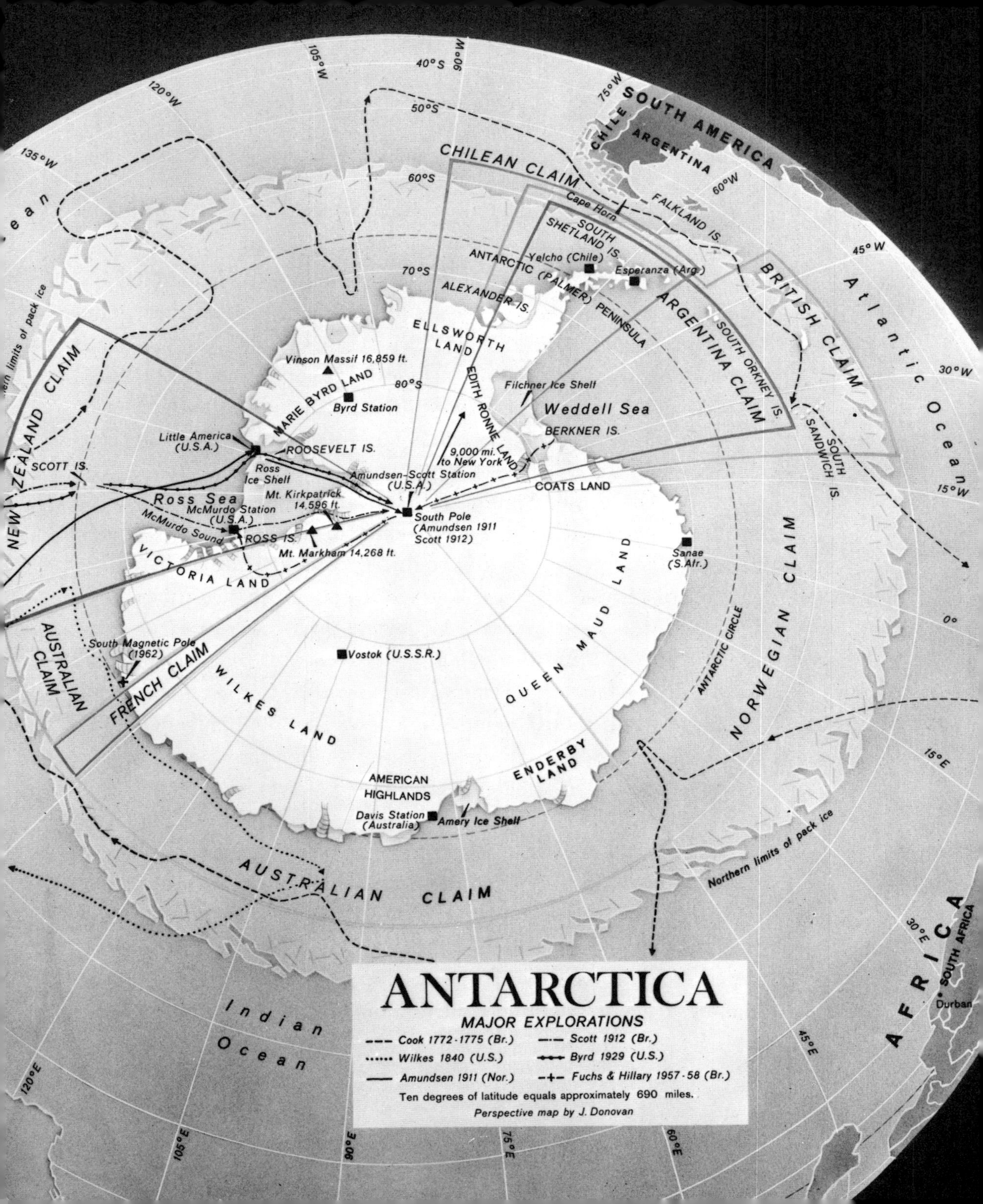
ANTARCTICA
MAJOR EXPLORATIONS
Cook 1772-1775 (Br.)
Wilkes 1840 (U.S.)
Amundsen 1911 (Nor.)
Scott 1912 (Br.)
Byrd 1929 (U.S.)
Fuchs & Hillary 1957-58 (Br.)
Ten degrees of latitude equals approximately 690 miles.
Perspective map by J. Donovan
SOUTH AMERICA
CHILE
ARGENTINA
CHILEAN CLAIM
Cape Horn
FALKLAND IS.
SOUTH SHETLAND IS.
Yelcho (Chile)
Esperanza (Arg.)
ANTARCTIC (PALMER) PENINSULA
ALEXANDER IS.
ARGENTINA CLAIM
SOUTH ORKNEY IS.
BRITISH CLAIM
Atlantic Ocean
SOUTH SANDWICH IS.
ELLSWORTH LAND
EDITH RONNE LAND
Filchner Ice Shelf
Weddell Sea
BERKNER IS.
COATS LAND
Vinson Massif 16,859 ft.
MARIE BYRD LAND
Byrd Station
9,000 mi. to New York
Little America (U.S.A.)
ROOSEVELT IS.
Ross Ice Shelf
Amundsen-Scott Station (U.S.A.)
NEW ZEALAND CLAIM
SCOTT IS.
Ross Sea
Mt. Kirkpatrick 14,596 ft.
McMurdo Station (U.S.A.)
McMurdo Sound
ROSS IS.
South Pole (Amundsen 1911 Scott 1912)
Mt. Markham 14,268 ft.
VICTORIA LAND
Sanae (S.Afr.)
QUEEN MAUD LAND
NORWEGIAN CLAIM
ANTARCTIC CIRCLE
South Magnetic Pole (1962)
FRENCH CLAIM
AUSTRALIAN CLAIM
Vostok (U.S.S.R.)
WILKES LAND
ENDERBY LAND
AMERICAN HIGHLANDS
Davis Station (Australia)
Amery Ice Shelf
Northern limits of pack ice
AUSTRALIAN CLAIM
Indian Ocean
AFRICA
SOUTH AFRICA
Durban
40°S
50°S
60°S
70°S
80°S
135°W
120°W
105°W
90°W
75°W
60°W
45°W
30°W
15°W
0°
15°E
30°E
45°E
60°E
75°E
90°E
105°E
120°E

invite the greater cooperation of their governments by so honoring the heads of state.

It would mean more to posterity and future explorers if names that were truly descriptive of the place were given to all geographic features. For example, a mountain peak named Cloud Maker by Shackleton, the Bay of Whales by Byrd, or even more descriptive, Desolation Island and Disappointment Bay are all very apt names. Explorers are responsible to and indebted to many individuals, companies, and nations, and it is understandable that they should wish to repay such indebtedness by leaving their patron's name on charts for generations to come.

In 1939 the United States set up a board on geographical names in the Department of Interior. Names to appear on U.S. charts were to be approved by this board. A committee established by this board created a policy to guide American cartographers and U.S. explorers. The policy recognized three categories of geographic features: those which give Antarctica its major characteristics, such as mountain ranges, seas, plateaus, and sections of the continent itself; those features such as small mountain ranges, unusual mountains, islands, gulfs, straits, and harbors; and finally, minor features such as cliffs, small capes, glaciers, anchorages, and so on.

Not only did the board set up these three categories of features, but they listed for guidance those for whom these features could be named. In the first class of major features the board determined that they should be named for expedition leaders, organizers of expeditions or patrons of one, a ship captain, or an individual making a major scientific contribution to mankind. The features

A view of exposed rock on the Bellingshausen Sea coast in eastern Antarctica. Photo was taken from a Navy helicopter. (US Navy)

in the second category could be named for ship captains, individuals performing acts of heroism, institutions, companies or individuals who have contributed to the expedition, and other members of an exploring party. The final category of features may be named for individuals who in any manner have contributed to an expedition and for almost any individual the expedition leader wishes to honor.

Among some of the more notable explorers in Antarctica who have left their names for the charts are Sir James Clark Ross (Ross Ice Shelf and Ross Sea), Roald Amundsen (Amundsen Sea), Lieutenant Charles Wilkes (Wilkes Land), Captain James Weddell (Weddell Sea), Rear Admiral R. E. Byrd (Marie Byrd Land, for his wife), Lincoln Ellsworth (Ellsworth Highland), and Captain Fabian Bellingshausen (Bellingshausen Sea).

Royalty, too, has left its imprint on major or first-order categories in Victoria Land, Queen Maud Land, Queen Mary Coast, Princess Ragnhild Coast, Princess Astrid Coast, Prince Olav Coast, Wilhelm II Coast, and Peter I Island.

Explorers also had a penchant for naming features after their ships. Mounts Erebus and Terror are two such, named for Captain Ross's ships during his expedition of 1839–43. Lieutenant Shirase named a portion of the coast Hainan Land, after his vessel *Hainan Maru*.

To list all of the geographic features named by individual explorers would be dull reading because of the vast number. For example, Captain Ronne on his expedition to the Palmer Peninsula gave names to eighty features that have been approved by the U.S. Board on Geographic Names!

Who Owns Antarctica?

In 1924 the United States government, through its State Department, made known to the world its position on unexplored and uninhabited lands. The American position was that mere discovery of a land is not enough to establish a claim to the land — it must be permanently settled by a nation before it can be claimed.

Before the International Geophysical Year in 1957, seven governments claimed portions of Antarctica. They were: Argentina, Australia, Chile, France, New Zealand, Norway, and Great Britain. Three of these claims overlapped — those of Argentina, Chile, and New Zealand. The United States had made no claim to any of the great continent, but put itself on record as not recognizing the claim of the other countries. The United States further stated that inasmuch as expeditions under its own government had explored more of Antarctica than any other nation, it might, in the future, have some claim of its own.

In 1958, when it became apparent that various nations intended to maintain permanent stations, the President of the United States called a conference with eleven other interested nations to work out a treaty for the area.

The resulting Antarctic Treaty was finally ratified in 1961. Among the provisions of the treaty are several articles concerning the use of the land and its ownership. The treaty does not affect the status of any nation's claim to certain areas, but it provides that any explorations taking place while the treaty is in effect can be used as a basis for additional claims. It advocates cooperation among the nations and exchange of scientific information.

Military bases are prohibited, although the military forces of a country can support the activities of peaceful expeditions. No nuclear explosions are permitted nor can there be any testing of weapons or training of military personnel on the continent.

To ensure that nations live up to the articles of this treaty, any nation may send inspectors to any other nation's base of activity. Historic sites, such as Scott's hut and Shackleton's hut on Evans Point are protected, as is the wildlife. In fact, the whole of the continent is designated as a vast conservation area.

Admiral Byrd, who hoped Antarctica would be known as the continent of peace, would have been pleased with the territorial cooperation in Antarctica today.

The International Geophysical Year

The year 1957–58 was selected as the International Geophysical Year because sunspot activity would reach its peak during that time. This meant that geophysicists of every nation would be greatly interested in what would take place in the upper atmosphere. The worldwide effort to collect information was coordinated by the International Council of Scientific Unions. The honorary chairman of the United States committee was Admiral

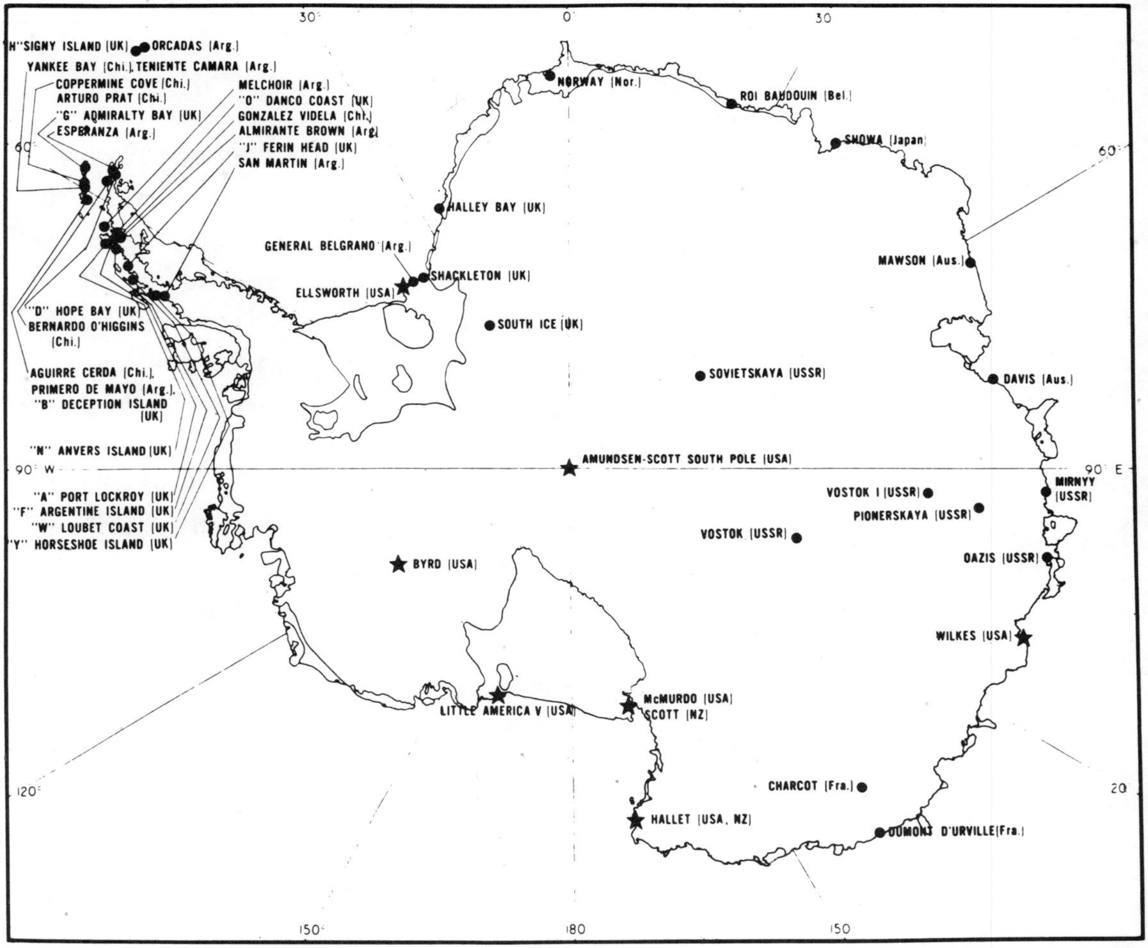

Antarctic stations during the International Geophysical Year.

Byrd; the chairman was Dr. Lawrence Gould, the chief scientist of Byrd's 1928–30 expedition.

Twelve nations agreed to that part of the program scheduled for Antarctica. They agreed to establish over sixty stations, including stations in the interior of the continent, where only Admiral Byrd had previously spent a winter. The United States Navy was given the job of supplying and supporting the American effort. The operation was nicknamed Deep Freeze I, and the navy poured ships, men, and airplanes into the continent to establish stations required by the scientists. When the IGY began, on July 1, 1957, the scientists were ready. It was fortunate that planning had been so complete, because a few days before this date, sunspots on the surface of the sun indicated that numerous gigantic explosions were taking place, the effects of which would be felt on earth.

Upon the successful completion of the IGY, enthusiastic scientists prevailed on their governments to pursue research in Antarctica on a continuing basis. The International Council of Scientific Unions established a permanent committee named Scientific Committee on Antarctic Research. This committee develops broad programs for research and investigations year after year. These long-range programs have no completion date, which shows that all nations expect the Antarctic to be occupied permanently.

Some Results of the IGY

Admiral Richard E. Byrd once wrote: " I am hopeful that Antarctica, in its symbolic robe of white, will shine forth as a continent of peace, as nations working together there in the cause of science set an example of international cooperation."

Above, a view of the Russian station Mirny in Antarctica. Below, the British base "Foxtro" on the Palmer Peninsula. (US Navy)

Byrd, with his vision and foresight, would have been pleased with the spirit of cooperation existing among the scientific and military groups living and working on the white continent under the continuing IGY program.

The IGY started with a veritable bang when sunspots on the surface of the sun showed interesting developments that led to one of the greatest magnetic storms ever recorded. Scientists all over the world, particularly in the Antarctic, gathered a mass of data that led to a fuller explanation of the effect of the sun's activity on the earth's radio waves. At America's polar station, at the geographic South Pole, one of the missions was to study the effect of the sun's activity on both the radio waves and the ionosphere that electrically charged the upper atmosphere some 50 to 250 miles above the earth. Scientists proved that this radio-reflecting band around the earth does not thin out or dissipate, though there are no direct sun's rays at the Pole for a period of six months. There were, however, some irregularities in the ionosphere that were recorded and have proven of great value to transpolar radio communication.

Seismologists, those scientists who study earth vibrations, have long wondered if even the delicate instruments they use would not be cushioned by the thousands of feet of snow in Antarctica and prevent readings being taken of distant earth tremors. Their doubts were put aside, however, when a recording was made of a tremor whose focal point was on the Kamchatka Peninsula, 9,900 miles away!

Nowhere in the world is there a better field laboratory for the glaciologists than in Antarctica. During the IGY, these scientists took many core samples of the compacted snow and ice to great depths. Since each year's snowfall can be seen as a separate layer, such samples give many clues to the past history of the continent. Annual temperatures can be calculated. Dust particles and pollen were found in melted samples, and in some cases spores were cultivated and grew fungi! Such molds were made from spores centuries old.

The continuing IGY has provided a unique opportunity for geologists to study their particular field. While all of the geologists do not believe in the Gondwanaland Theory of continental drift,

A view of Byrd Station during the International Geophysical Year. (US Navy)

there is considerable evidence to support it. Geologists have studied glacial gravels, called tillites, to see whether these outcrops resemble those of Australia, South America, and Africa. They have geologically divided Antarctica into east and west and discovered that the two are different in some respects. For example, West Antarctica is very similar in geography to the lower end of South America, and the mountain ranges discovered are undoubtedly a continuation of the Andes Mountains of that continent. Huge quantities of coal have been located. Since coal is formed from a variety of plants, it is obvious that at some earlier time Antarctica was a continent of rain forests.

Oceanographers studying shellfish have discovered the remains of a freshwater species known to have lived 250 to 550 million years ago. They found these in a remote Antarctic mountain range. From such clues scientists hope to shed light on the evolution of life.

Biologists are also studying the evolution of life when they analyze the variegated contents of the oceans surrounding the white continent. Oceanographers assist and have verified a long-standing theory of how the cold, northward flowing currents affect the weather over much of the rest of the world.

All of the scientists cooperating in IGY and the subsequent years have contributed to man's knowledge. Much has been learned but much more is to be learned in the world's greatest laboratory of the past.

How Polar Explorers Keep Warm

A man would quickly freeze to death if he did not dress properly in the Antarctic. The Eskimos of the Arctic regions have lived for centuries in freezing climates, so polar explorers have borrowed much of their dress from them.

A polar explorer wears clothes that weigh from 12 to 15 pounds. If his clothing were any heavier it would be so bulky and clumsy he could not walk easily. Yet this clothing must be loose enough so that it does not restrict the explorer's circulation and must provide an air space between itself and his body. Warm air circulating in this air space acts as an insulator: it prevents cold air from the outside from coming in direct contact with the explorer's body.

The polar explorer's outside garment is a long, coatlike Eskimo parka with a hood on it. The parka reaches below his hips. The armholes are big enough so that he can pull his arms in and out of the sleeves and hold them against his body to warm them. At the neck, or around the hood, and at the waist there are drawstrings. When the drawstrings are pulled tight, the warm air between the explorer's body and his parka is prevented from escaping. Parkas are made of gabardine and other windproof materials as well as from animal skins. Early explorers thought reindeer skin most suitable for a parka because it is very light and warm.

A polar explorer's pants are made of skin or some waterproof material. Recent explorers have tried closely woven materials of

Parka covering his head, this Navy photographer wears a modern version of a balaclava, *or face mask, to protect his face against the bitter Antarctic winds. (US Navy)*

light weight that keep out both water and wind. Underneath his parka and pants an explorer wears loose woolen clothing.

Although the hood of his parka covers his head, an explorer also wears a *balaclava* for added warmth. This is a tight-fitting woolen cap made like a woolen sock with a hole in it for his face.

One's hands and feet can get frostbitten very easily in the Antarctic. Therefore, explorers take great care to keep them warm. To protect their hands in very cold weather they wear woolen gloves covered with heavy mittens made of caribou, wolfskin, or a synthetic material. They are very careful never to touch a piece of metal with their bare hands in these low temperatures. Their skin would freeze to the metal and pull away from the flesh. To protect their hands, scientists working with delicate instruments can wear tight silk gloves for a short while.

Explorers have difficulty protecting their feet on the trail in Antarctica. They wear Eskimo *kamids* and Siberian *mukluks.* These are fur boots. The kamid has a hard sole like ordinary shoes, so it is easier to walk in than the soft-soled mukluk. Modern boots are adapted from these early models.

Formerly, travelers in Antarctic regions padded the insides of their boots with *sennegrass,* a kind of grass that grows in Norway and other northern countries. Moisture from the feet collects and freezes into crystals on the grass. The crystals can be easily shaken off, leaving the grass dry again. Modern boots have inner liners to accomplish the same thing.

Despite their precautions, personnel working in Antarctic climates sometimes do get frostbitten. Frostbite occurs when any part of the body gets so cold that the blood will not circulate properly. Victims of frostbite must never use the old remedy of rubbing snow on cold parts of their bodies to warm them. That is very dangerous. Instead, they should warm the cold part with their hands until the blood starts circulating again.

Another painful hazard of Antarctic exploration is snow blindness, which is caused by the reflection of the sun on the snow. To prevent this condition explorers wear sunglasses.

When modern polar explorers have to spend the night on the trail, away from base camp, they must have protection against the wind and snow. They carry lightweight, windproof tents that are held up by bamboo or aluminum poles. These tents have a double entrance at one end. The men go in one doorway, then close it before they go through the second entrance to the tent. In this way they prevent snow from blowing into their sleeping quarters.

Explorers also use sleeping bags made of caribou skins or some waterproof material. Drawstrings close these man-size bags tight around the sleepers' necks to keep the warm air around their bodies from escaping.

Although tents are fine for a short sledging trip or for emergency use, the expedition must have a permanent, warm shelter during the long cold winter months from April to November. The houses that modern Antarctic explorers use are called huts. They are built in sections long before the expedition leaves on the trip south. These sections measure about 4 by 8 feet in size and are made of plywood, fiber glass, and aluminum. They are first put together in the factory to see that they fit exactly right, then they are taken apart and packed in large crates. They are packed so that the first section to be taken out of the crate is the first to be erected. As each part is unpacked, it is immediately put into place.

The huts for Byrd's Little America expedition were not built on top of the snow. First, the men dug a big square hole about 6 feet deep. At the bottom of the hole they laid the foundation for the hut. Over the foundation they laid the beams for the floor. The foundation was raised about 2 feet above the hole so that the floor would not rest on the ice and snow. When the men put the last section of the hut into place, they shoveled snow all around the outside walls up to the roof. The snow protected the hut from wind and driving snow and helped to keep it warm.

The windows of an Antarctic hut — whether in Byrd's time or

Modern, sectionalized construction of huts is now common in Antarctica. Above, Deep Freeze personnel put large Granco arches in place over the trench for the main tunnel at New Byrd Station. Below, a typical hut used by "wintering over" personnel, as seen during a 40-knot wind and driving snow. (US Navy)

today — are in the roof. They are so made that they can be raised above the snow that is bound to pile up on the roof. They work very much like the periscope of a submarine. Because it is too cold in the Antarctic to open the windows for fresh air, huts are equipped with ventilators that reach well up above the roof. Thus, nobody has to leave the warm hut to see what the weather is like outside. Each hut has a high tower with heavy glass windows. By climbing a ladder into the tower, the men can see whether it is clear or snowing.

Admiral Byrd connected each Antarctic hut to its neighbor with a tunnel made by digging a deep trench in the snow, stacking its sides with boxes of food and other supplies, and then laying a wooden frame across the top. On top of the frame, chicken wire and canvas were laid down for a roof. Then the snow that had been dug out was shoveled back on top. Byrd also designed special tunnels for dogs. They were made in the same way as the supply tunnels except that they were lined not by boxes of supplies but by doghouses. The doghouses were placed far enough apart so that when the dogs were chained to them they could not reach each other to fight.

Station-building in Antarctica has become a science since the International Geophysical Year. Permanent bases such as the McMurdo Station are almost little cities, but those out on the ice shelf or on the plateau are now designed as semipermanent. Byrd Station is built in trenches with prefabricated buildings set into them and covered with a steel-supported roof.

Amundsen-Scott South Pole Station was originally built on top of the snow in 1956. By 1963, however, all the buildings were

Right, a Peter snow miller at work digging trenches at New Byrd Station. Below, milled snow, called "Peter snow," is carried by chutes over the machine and deposited into the trench which the miller is digging. Snow then hardens to twice the strength of the original snow, thus making a support for arches used to cover the trenches. (US Navy)

completely covered with snow, and a new design of building, called the Wonder Arch, replaced the older buildings. In this type of construction, a deep trench is dug by a Peter snow plow, and steel arches are placed over the trench. This ice and steel construction provides a covered area, into which prefabricated buildings are placed and joined together.

McMurdo Station is built largely on a rock base and the metal buildings are similar to those used in various other parts of the world. All of them have to be well insulated against the cold. In building the nuclear power plant at McMurdo Sound it was necessary to dig down into the bedrock to place the reactor containment vessels. This required many hours of hard, cold work.

The Food Antarctic Explorers Eat

For any expedition to withstand the rigors of a prolonged stay in the Antarctic, it is imperative that food consumption be given a high degree of intelligent planning. Expedition medical officers, armed with the modern advances of medical science, have combined to produce minimum requirements for explorers. The diet of every member of an expedition must contain all the proteins, calories, minerals, and vitamins required by the human body. Because of the severe conditions imposed by this inhospitable land, careful attention to the selection, transportation, and preparation of all foods is an absolute necessity.

While a hardworking man at home in temperate climates can live well on 4,500 calories per day, an explorer needs at least 5,500 calories to produce the same energy. These calories must be obtained through a daily diet that is properly balanced with carbohydrates, fats, and protein. Both carbohydrates and protein will yield about 113 calories per ounce, and fats about 255 calories per ounce. It is also important to ensure that this proper balance will contain the right amounts of calcium, phosphorus, iron, copper, and iodine.Most balanced diets will include these minerals in sufficient quantities.

This is not true of the vitamins. These highly active chemical agents are not always present or are destroyed in storage or cooking. Vitamins A, B complex, C, and D are absolutely necessary in the diet and must be augmented by taking a synthetic form of them to ensure that all the needs are met.

Carbohydrates consumed are generally in the form of fruit or vegetable products. Fats are obtained from suet, milk products, and fish-liver oils. Proteins are available in vegetables (green leaf), whole-grain cereals, and beans; the most valuable proteins are those furnished by meat, milk, and eggs. Rich sources of natural vitamins are kidney, liver, eggs, and milk products.

The importance of vitamins has long been recognized by explorers and seafaring men, with the most dramatic disease caused by vitamin deficiency being scurvy. Fortunately, medical science has been able to define the source of all the vitamins and man's average requirement. Careful planning of a person's diet is generally all that is required to ensure his well-being.

While out on the trail, hot meals are difficult to obtain because of the problem of food preparation. There is also a need for weight reduction in the amount of food that can be carried. Explorers have known for many years that the mainstay of any trail travel, by sledge or skis, is pemmican.

Dr. Dana Coman has prepared the following diet as one entirely satisfactory for hard sledge travel in cold weather.

Trail rations, approximately 37 ounces per man per day:

	Ounces
Pemmican	12
Biscuit	6
Bacon	1
Butter	2
Oatmeal	2½
Whole-milk powder	4
Lump sugar	2
Milk chocolate	4
Fruit (dry and powdered)	1
Orange or lemon powder	¾
Peanuts or almonds	1
Cocoa	¾
Salt and pepper	1/10

Traveling in Antarctica

An explorer in the Antarctic region faces the toughest traveling in the world. He must be prepared to move over ice so slippery and hard that he cannot stand up on it. He must clear a trail in the fine-grained snow before he can travel through it. At times there is a hard crust on the snow. At other times there is knee-deep slush to wade through. The surface of the ice and snow is crisscrossed by crevasses. These are often hidden by snow bridges that cave in under a man's weight.

The snow-and-ice-bound surface of Antarctica is rarely smooth. It is scarred by "pressure ridges" — ragged walls built up by snow and ice under pressure. It is often marred by *sastrugi* — wave-like irregularities set up on the surface by the wind. Sometimes there are potholes covered by a thin crust of snow. It is dangerous to travel on foot without skis.

Explorers have tried many different means of transportation: dogs, ponies, snowmobiles, tractors, "weasels" — the army's amphibious boats with treads — airplanes, and within the last two decades, helicopters.

Tractors, snowmobiles, and weasels have treads like those of an army tank. The treads give them a flat surface to roll on. They also keep the vehicles from sinking into the snow, and they pull without slipping. They are used to haul big, heavy sleds with wide runners. Often they tow airplanes over the snow to the runways.

Helicopters are used for rescue work and short exploring trips. They have proved their value many times over. They can be flown

Trail blazing in an Antarctic crevasse area. Vehicle is a highly successful weasel crevasse detector. Flags mark safe trail for other vehicles to follow. (US Navy)

from the deck of a ship and therefore need no long runway for takeoff. Their principal disadvantage is that they are difficult to handle in a high wind.

Most of the surveying and mapping in the Antarctic is done by airplane. In earlier days it took explorers a whole summer season to map a limited area. Today they photomap that same area in one day, traveling by air.

Some planes in the polar regions are equipped with skis to land on the ice or snow, and with pontoons to land on the water. But flying in the below-zero temperatures of the Antarctic is no fun. Oil in the engine of a propeller-driven plane will get as thick as tar if the plane is left standing in temperatures 40 degrees below zero. The engine must be drained of oil after each flight. When the mechanics prepare the plane for takeoff they have to warm the oil on a stove before they pour it into the engine. Then they have to warm the engine itself with hot-air blowers before it will start.

Usually the plane's skis are frozen to the runway and the pilot must break them out before he can taxi the plane. Then, while he

Tractors, called Snow Cats, pulled sledges like these for the Fuchs-Hillary Trans-Antarctic Expedition of 1958. The vehicles made a historic 950-mile traverse to the South Pole Station from the Weddell Sea coast. (US Navy)

Photographed against the rising slopes of the Antarctic highlands is a weasel towing two heavy cargo sleds. (US Navy)

is warming up the engine, the skis may freeze to the runway again before he can get the plane moving. It takes two hours or more to get a plane ready to fly in the polar regions. The weather that was good when the pilot started readying the plane for flight may be terrible when he is set to take off.

No matter what other kind of transportation explorers take with them, they will need sleds — or sledges as they are usually called.

The runners of the sledge must be wide enough so that they will not sink into the snow, but not wide enough to make the sledge hard to pull. The sledge itself must be wide enough so that it will not tip over easily with a load, and the framework that holds the "bed," or carrying part of the sledge, must be high enough not to drag in the deep snow.

One of the sledges used by the Bryd expedition was 9½ feet long and 25 inches wide, with 4-inch-wide runners. The whole sledge, even the runners, was made of strong hickory wood.

Big trains of sledges carry a caboose called a wanigan. The wanigan is really a house on sled runners for the sledging party to live in on the trail. The name "wanigan" comes from an Indian word meaning "trap." Lumbermen first used it as a name for a houseboat carrying supplies.

Traditional dog teams of huskies are still used in Antarctica. This particular team, waiting for its master to return, is used to haul men and cargo short distances around McMurdo Station. (US Navy)

A C-130 Hercules cargo plane loads up on a sea-ice runway, as New Zealand dog handlers from Scott Base, Ross Island, exercise their dog teams at McMurdo Sound air facility. (US Navy)

In the last decade, not only the United States but other nations interested in Antarctica have tried different types of aircraft and land equipment.

The C-130 turboprop transport has been America's workhorse as far as transporting cargo is concerned. While it can land on snow and ice runways, it can also land on unimproved snow surfaces. It regularly flies airdrop, search and rescue, and photographic missions. For purposes of flying in personnel from the rest of the world, the Super Constellation, with its wheeled tricycle landing gear, has been used extensively. This huge plane normally lands on snow and ice runways especially prepared for such heavy aircraft.

Earlier helicopters used for ice reconnaissance, flown from icebreakers and other ships, are being rapidly replaced by turbine-equipped types that can range farther and carry greater loads. Among such newer helicopters are the Sikorsky CH-19 and HH-52, and the Kaman UH-2B.

Two types of helicopters used for land exploration and transportation in near-to-remote areas are the LH-34 flown by the navy, and the Bell UH-1, an army helicopter. The UH-1 can be carried inside the C-130 planes.

Navy helicopter waits in the background as its crew, assigned to a Deep Freeze unit, check a giant "grasshopper" device used to transmit radio signal weather reports. (US Navy)

Whales

There are two kinds of whales — those that have teeth and those that do not. Those with no teeth have instead a sieve of whalebone called baleen, through which they strain food out of the sea. The giant blue whale and the fin whale are both baleen whales. The blue is sometimes 150 feet long and weighs approximately 150 tons.

In the cold waters around the Antarctic ice pack there are areas of red-colored seawater. These areas, sometimes miles wide, are red because they are filled with billions of tiny shrimplike organisms known as krill. This is the food of the baleen whales. One of them can easily consume 2,000 pounds of krill a day.

The sperm whale is a member of the family of whales having teeth. In fact, the sperm has more than twenty pairs of teeth in its lower jaw. Usually the sperm will not fight, but sometimes when he is harpooned he will attack a boat.

Even so, the sperm is as gentle as a lamb compared to the killer whale. Near the Antarctic ice pack there are thousands of killer whales. They roam the icy waters in bands, sometimes only a few together, sometimes as many as a hundred. As whales go, the killers are small — perhaps 25 feet long and weighing 15 tons. While that is three times as big as an African elephant, the actual size is small compared to the giant 150-ton blue whale.

No animal in the world can compare with a killer whale in fierceness. Two killers can kill a blue whale ten times their size. Strangely enough, they kill the big fellow by drowning him. A

Killer whales are comparatively small — only about 25 feet in length. This one was photographed in captivity at Marineland of the Pacific. (Courtesy, Marineland of the Pacific, Los Angeles)

blue whale can hold its breath under water for only five minutes, but a killer can hold his for about twenty minutes. Two killers grab the lower jaw of a blue, one on each side. Then they hold his head under until he drowns. When the blue is dead, the killers cut out his tongue with their huge teeth. The tongue is all they eat because even their three-inch-long teeth cannot puncture the tough, one-inch-thick hide of the blue.

Killers can stand on their tails and stick their heads out of the water about 8 feet. On one Antarctic expedition a driver and his dogs were on the ice near the ship when the driver saw a pack of killers standing on their tails and looking at him over the edge of the ice. He headed for heavier ice in a hurry, but suddenly the ice under him began to heave and crack. The killers had dived under the 2½ feet of ice and were breaking it with their backs. Wherever cracks appeared, they stood on their tails to see which way the driver and the dogs were headed. Fortunately, the driver reached the heavier ice and was saved.

Seals

There are six kinds of seals in Antarctic waters today. At one time there were many fur seals, but at the beginning of the last century, hunters with no thought for preserving the species killed them all. Today, explorers kill seals only for dog food and, in emergencies, for themselves if they need fresh meat.

One kind of seal is called the elephant seal because he has a trunk about 10 inches long. A blow on his sensitive trunk will knock him unconscious.

Elephant seals are the largest of all seals. They are hunted for the oil that can be obtained from the thick blubbery fat that coats their bodies.

The crabeater seal is all white and spends his whole life floating around on ice pans. His favorite food is the small octopus that lives in the water near the ice pack.

The green-bellied seal has a thick, loose-skinned neck. To protect himself in a fight with another seal, he can pull his head clear down into his neck.

Near Little America is a colony of Weddell seals. Thousands of them live in the caves and crevasses of the ice. The young seal

A Weddell seal on the sea ice near McMurdo Station, Antarctica. (US Navy)

pups are born in October of each year. When they are about two weeks old, their mothers give them swimming lessons because they are not born with the ability to swim.

Scientists and divers have had an opportunity to study the habits of the Weddell seals near the ice-pack edge. It has been determined that they can dive through a hole in the ice pack to a depth of perhaps 2,000 feet, and with a built-in navigating system, return to the same hole after having been under water for forty minutes.

Fish and Other Sea Life

Some fish of the cod family are caught around Antarctica, and some that have never been seen anywhere else in the world. One, found in the Ross Sea, has a body as transparent as glass, with a tiny tail, two black fins, and black eyes.

There are also starfish and a kind of octopus around the ice pack, and a few fish familiar to the water of our own continent. Although there are no sea snakes, there is a very ugly sea worm about 20 inches long. And there are eels that have no heads.

Among the different types of sea life identified in Antarctic waters are many which are quite unusual. One animal, called a hydroid, looks like and is often mistaken for seaweed. Other life includes sea urchins, sea cucumbers, feather stars, and starfish.

Penguins, Petrels, and Other Birds

There are no polar bears in the Antarctic. In fact, there are no four-legged animals at all. But there are many penguins.

The emperor penguins are the largest. They are 3 to 4 feet tall and weigh from 60 to 70 pounds. With their black coats and yellow breasts, they look very dignified. When they waddle around in their normal upright position, they look as though they were

A superb photo of an emperor penguin, over three feet in height. A penguin chick peers between its mother's feet. (US Navy)

strutting. The emperors fear neither men nor dogs. In fact, they will sometimes attack a man with their beaks and short flippers.

The Adélie penguins are smaller than the emperors — only about 18 inches tall. They have black coats and white vests. Their heads look like black helmets with white eyeholes.

Adélies are the most inquisitive birds in the world. They will investigate anything they see. During the naval expedition in 1946–47 known as Operation Highjump, an Adélie jumped out of the water onto the deck of the submarine *Sennet,* whereupon he walked toward the conning tower and bowed formally to the commanding officer. For thirty-six hours he hitchhiked aboard the submarine, investigating everything on deck, cocking his head sideways when something puzzled him.

The penguins' chief enemy is the sea leopard, a killer seal that hunts near penguin colonies. Before a penguin dives into the water in search of food, he stands on the edge of the ice and looks the water over carefully for the shadow of his enemy. If there is more than one penguin on the ice, the one about to dive will try to push one of his friends into the water first to see if it is safe.

Female penguins build their nests of small round stones on the ground in big community nesting places known as rookeries. They do not hatch their eggs by sitting on them but by holding them on top of their webbed feet and pressing them up against their stomachs.

If a mother penguin loses her chick she tries to kidnap one from another mother. If she does not succeed, she finds a small round stone and treats it as she would an egg.

The male penguins bring food to the mother birds until the

chicks are hatched. Then both parents take turns watching the babies. Penguins are such good mothers that even if they are buried in the snow by a blizzard they will not desert their eggs or their chicks.

An Adélie penguin is faithful to its mate, and each year the same pair returns to the nest they built the year before to hatch another egg. Since the grown birds have few enemies on the ice or land, they sleep almost anyplace, sometimes standing up with their bill tucked under a flipper, or they may even lie down. While pen-

An Adélie penguin with her two baby chicks at Cape Crozier, Antarctica. (US Navy)

guins are very curious and not afraid of men, they are afraid of loud noises; therefore pilots have been instructed to avoid flying over rookeries.

The little chicks' greatest enemies are the skua gulls. These dangerous birds have a 4-foot wingspread, and they have been known to attack a man. Sometimes two skua gulls will simultaneously attack one mother penguin. When she turns her back on her chick to attack one of the gulls, the other grabs the helpless baby.

After the young penguins are about half grown, they are placed in nurseries with several penguin nurses to look after them while the mothers and fathers look for food. If one of the young birds wanders away from the nursery, a nurse slaps him back into the circle with her flippers.

At last the young penguins go to sea. Sometimes they are in such a hurry to get down to the water that they flop over onto their stomachs and slide along like sleds, pushing themselves with their flippers. They are fine swimmers and they have no trouble getting back onto the ice when they want to; in fact, they can leap 8 feet out of the water.

The giant petrel, or fulmar, is a bird with a 7-foot wingspread. He is like a vulture, for he eats the carcasses of dead animals. Often he stuffs himself with food until he is too heavy to fly.

Other petrels in Antarctica are the silver-gray and the stormy petrels. The last are sometimes called Mother Carey's chickens.

The prettiest of all petrels is the snow-white ice petrel. His feathers look like white satin. He has jet-black eyes and a black bill. Snow petrels fly farther inland than any of the other birds.

They have been seen 150 miles inland and at altitudes of 6,000 feet.

Among the smaller birds are the whalebirds, the small gray prions, and the terns. The whalebird is really a petrel. He gets his name from the fact that he has a sieve in his mouth through which he strains food out of the sea, just as the giant blue whale does.

Index